Tikkun Olam
& Other Poems

by

Leo Yankevich

Books by Leo Yankevich

Collections
The Unfinished Crusade
The Last Silesian

Chapbooks
The Language of Birds
Grief's Herbs (after Stanisław Grochowiak)
The Gnosis of Gnomes
Epistle from the Dark
The Golem of Gleiwitz

E-Books
Metaphysics
"You Who Live and Hear"
Tikkun Olam (first edition)

TIKKUN OLAM
& OTHER POEMS

SECOND, EXPANDED EDITION

by

Leo Yankevich

Foreword by E. M. Schorb

Counter-Currents Publishing Ltd.
San Francisco
2012

Copyright © 2012 Leo Yankevich
All rights reserved

Some of these poems have been published in the following publications, to whose editors grateful acknowledgement is made:
Chronicles, Contemporary Sonnet, Counter-Currents, CounterPunch, Iambs & Trochees, The MacGuffin, Mandrake Poetry Review, The New Formalist, The Pennsylvania Review, Poets Against War, The Raintown Review, The Susquehanna Quarterly, Trinacria, Visions International, War Poetry, and *Washington Literary Review.*

Cover design by Kevin I. Slaughter

Published in the United States by
COUNTER-CURRENTS PUBLISHING LTD.
P.O. Box 22638
San Francisco, CA 94122
USA
http://www.counter-currents.com/

Second Edition

Hardcover ISBN: 978-1-935965-37-4
Paperback ISBN: 978-1-935965-38-1
E-book ISBN: 978-1-935965-39-8

For Aleksandr Solzhenitsyn

Contents

Foreword by E. M. Schorb ♦ 1

Part One

1. Tikkun Olam ♦ 5
2. Moscow, 1928 ♦ 6
3. Holodomor, 1932–1933 ♦ 7
4. Red Star, 1933 ♦ 8
5. Barcelona, 1936 ♦ 9
6. Naftaly Aronovich Frenkel ♦ 10
7. Kolyma, 1937 ♦ 13
8. Lorca's Death ♦ 14

Part Two

9. Neighbours, Eastern Poland, 1940 ♦ 17
10. December, 1942 ♦ 18
11. Vengeance is Mine, Says the Lord, 1943 ♦ 20
12. With Blood on his Hands, Commissar Y. Raichman Ponders the Forest of the Dead at Katyn, 1943 ♦ 21
13. Koniuchy, Eastern Poland, 1944 ♦ 22
14. Saint Bartholomew's Church ♦ 23
15. Gleiwitz, 1945 ♦ 25
16. Somewhere over Germany, 1945 ♦ 26
17. Veteran's Hospital ♦ 27

Part Three

18. After the Expulsions ♦ 31
19. Ezra Pound Enters the Tent ♦ 32
20. Dissident, 1962 ♦ 33
21. Poland, New Year's Day, 1982 ♦ 34
22. A Hater Learns About Love ♦ 35
23. The Loneliest Man ♦ 36
24. The Death of Communism ♦ 38
25. Bukovina, 1989 ♦ 41

Part Four

26. Sarajevo Sonnet ♦ 43
27. Draza Bregovich ♦ 44
28. Epiphany ♦ 45
29. Elegy ♦ 46
30. Butugychag ♦ 47
31. Gulag Burial Marker ♦ 48
32. The Abandoned Station ♦ 49
33. The Last Silesian ♦ 50
34. An Interview with the Oldest Man In Europe ♦ 51
35. The *Łemko* Steeple ♦ 52
36. Starless ♦ 53

Part Five

37. A Plurality of Worlds ♦ 57
38. Water ♦ 58
39. The Poet of 1912 ♦ 59
40. Anonymous Rex ♦ 60
41. How to Get There ♦ 61

Part Six

42. Spreading Democracy ♦ 65
43. Jenin, 2002 ♦ 67
44. The Terrorist ♦ 68
45. After the Old Masters ♦ 69
46. No Flowers, No Doves ♦ 70
47. Two Dates ♦ 71
48. On the Beheading of Eugene Olin Armstrong ♦ 72
49. The July Sun over Lebanon ♦ 73
50. On the Lynching of Saddam Hussein ♦ 74
51. Black Ops ♦ 76

Part Seven

52. A Warning to Dissidents ♦ 79
53. Halloween, 2006 ♦ 80
54. The Condemned House ♦ 81
55. Understanding the Holocaust ♦ 82
56. Vision ♦ 83
57. Monomatapa on the Detroit River ♦ 84

Epilogue

58. Epilogue ♦ 87

About the Author ♦ 89

FOREWORD

Reading the powerful, ironic poems in *Tikkun Olam*—Hebrew for "the mending of the world"—in this new enlarged edition, visions of Goya's *Disasters of War* come to mind.

Leo Yankevich wants the truth—wants it out—and uses all his considerable power as a poet to get it out, bitter and bittersweet. Santayana said, "Those who do not remember the past are condemned to repeat it." Yankevich wants us to remember the past, so that we need not repeat it. Is this a futile dream? But someone must do something to halt or at least to slow our simian march to doom, and Yankevich does what he can in this dark true book.

The murderous, testosterone-drugged alpha males portrayed in *Tikkun Olam* are not utter monsters. They are humans—husbands, sons, and brothers. They are us, or parts of us, and it is their residual humanity that is horrifying.

This is especially clear when Yankevich takes on infamously unattractive personalities and manages to find in them the germ of humanity that is just alive enough to make stark and painful how much of their humanity has been cast off. His portrait of Rudolf Hess comes to mind. I think, too, of those menders of the world who begin their mending with the murders of the Tsar, his wife and children.

Tikkun Olam is filled with characters—human, all too human, not quite human, alive and suffering in their various tragedies—brought painfully and beautifully to life by Leo Yankevich.

E. M. Schorb

PART ONE

TIKKUN OLAM*
Ekaterinburg, Russia,
17 July 1918

His mouth agape, as though still asking questions,
the Tsar lies at the end of his long reign.
(Blue lips almost struggle to explain,
caught in the halfway realm of last expressions.)

The Empress sprawls, hands crossing her stained bodice.
Behind her rest the bayoneted heirs,
blood in pools around their jewelled stares.
Yurovsky stands above the heap of bodies.

A Chekist practiced in the art of killing,
he commends his men as gun smoke settles.
Their trigger-fingers, though, are cocked and curled,

their executioner eyes more than willing—
all of them, like him, poor boys from shtetls,
still eager to help mend the broken world.

*Hebrew for "the mending of the world."

MOSCOW, 1928
Those Who Would Dare Speak the Truth

Through iron bars and sooty glass,
you see a square of muddy snow,
where cawing rooks and jackdaws pass
over the heads of those who go
no further than the prison walls—
mothers, fathers, weeping wives
bearing bags of fruit and rolls
to those whose candour cost their lives.

HOLODOMOR, 1932-1933

The golden wheat of the Ukraine
rots in a packed-to-the-brim silo.
Nearby, a Chekist bashes the brain
of a Kulak, as in a sideshow
historians agree to forget.

Tomorrow his gaunt wife will feed
her drumstick children acacia flowers
or sparrows crushed beneath her feet.
The following day she'll beg the powers-
that-be for a stale loaf of bread.

And the day after that she'll lie
cradling moons. Among the rich,
she will not feel starvation's bite,
nor Lazar's wrath inside the ditch
with the forsaken and the dead.

Red Star, 1933

The Arctic wind impales us without halt
and in our wounds the devil himself leers.
The star above the gulag burns like salt
until we lose all track of months and years.

And yet we sigh again the wry insult
we let slip into Comrade Stalin's ears.
We sigh until we sigh it by default
and wrinkles are the riverbeds of tears.

BARCELONA, 1936

Perhaps there's mercy in the skies,
although the Spaniards have seen none.
The tears of horror in their eyes
reflect the fury of the sun
lifting the curtain over dawn.
They know that Orlov's Reds were there:
a priest lies bludgeoned on the lawn,
and Christian Spain lies struck at prayer.

NAFTALY ARONOVICH FRENKEL
Architect of the Gulag System

For Robert Conquest

I.

Each day Naftaly greets a prison train.
Two days ago: spies and reactionaries,
yesterday: Kulaks from Ukraine,
this morning: counter-revolutionaries.

Snug in his fur behind militia guards
who hold thick water hoses in the snow,
he looks at blue-lipped prisoners in cars,
exposed to frost of twenty-five below.

He tells the "fascist cattle" to undress
because they're going "to take nice warm baths."
"Enjoy this hot Siberian steam," he says,
then slams the door. Behind it, no one laughs.

Not the young mother and her infant son,
not the old teacher leaning on his cane,
not the wry poet and the tender nun
whose final prayers and tears are frozen rain.

II.

Only the strong make it to Magadan
to labour for a crumb or crust of bread,
a spoon of fish-bone soup. Tonight each man
is one of many pillars that must tread

through ice and snow from toil in the mines.
Now they rest in the barracks. Half are gone,
completely at odds with their freezing minds,
and half won't live to see the light of dawn.

Together they stand, leaning up along
the walls to shore the gaping holes and cracks.
The weakest are supported by the strong,
those who wear rags and old potato sacks.

And every now and then one hears a cry,
not of agony,—but of despair,
as time and justice pass the pillars by
and barracks dim with each forsaken prayer.

III.

And when I look down at the crimson map
I see the countless trains in permafrost,
and I see Frenkel, the star on his cap
above the twenty million who were lost.

I hear the broken Russian in each command;
The pillars and barracks rise up from the page
of the great Atlas, and I understand
the architecture of that place and age.

Kolyma, 1937

I see your noble face behind barbed wire,
looking out at endless taiga, greeted
only by cold. The laughter of the liar
who put you there is still loud in your ears,
although in far-off Moscow now—he's seated,
the hooked-nosed slayer of the highborn rich,
sadist and defiler of Slavic daughters,
egalitarian savant and snitch.

Who do you think will recall the martyrs,
the frightened faces and the countless tears,
the forgotten dead of Russia and Ukraine?
Who will write the history of their pain?
"You who live and hear," your voice falters,
still so frightened after all these years.

Lorca's Death

Spain, nineteen thirty-seven.
We pass five graves: a nun,
four altar boys who'd done
nothing to enter heaven

decades before their time,
but be the victims of rape.
Red bullets, crimson tape,
are bedfellows to the crime.

A black patch on one eye,
Fernando coughs to begin.
Grief burns his cheeks and chin,
and then he tells me why.

I swear I can still hear
his voice amid my thoughts:
"For this we fired two shots
into the faggot's rear."

Part Two

Neighbours Eastern Poland, 1940

I turn my shoulder to the grey and think
of Yosel, son of Saul Rabinsky, how
he slammed the doors of crowded cattle cars
bound for Siberia, although the faces
inside were those of neighbours, Catholic Poles.

How haplessly they looked back through the cracks,
their petty gentry voices cursing him
and the red star on his cone-shaped traitor's cap,
their love of Poland beyond his comprehension,
their foolishness not worthy of his grief.

He did not know few would survive the journey
and those who did would perish in the gulags,
their tundra-bitten bodies heaped beneath
Lavrentii Beria's orders, like forgotten
enemies of a freedom-loving state.

The son of Saul Rabinsky did not know
the Wehrmacht would attack within a year
and soon behind them come a death's head squad
to mock the bearded rabbis of the town
and herd its Jews into a killing field.

He did not know he'd be betrayed by neighbours,
who, in a cabal of silence and revenge,
would watch the gendarmes drag him through the square,
neighbours with whom he'd played and gone to school

and whose unbridled hatred matched his own.

DECEMBER, 1942
After Peter Huchel

How resounding is the winter squall.
Hole-riddled the loam walls of Bethlehem's stall.

That's Mary murdered at the entrance gate,
Hair frozen to the bloody stones and grate.

Masked in rags, three soldiers limping by
Cannot burn from her ear the infant's cry.

The last canteen sunflower won't get them far.
They seek the way and cannot see the star.

Aurum, thus, myrrham offerunt . . .
Crow and cur come to a manger ruined.

. . . *quia natus est nobis Dominus.*
On a bleached skeleton gleam soot and ooze.

The way to Stalingrad's a smouldering glow.
And it leads to a charnel house of snow.

Vengeance is Mine, Says the Lord, 1943

In memory of the German and Russian soldiers buried together in mass graves during the battle of Stalingrad.

If but the sun had burned less brightly
upon the faces of the dead
He saw heaped high that winter day
inside a pit dug in a field,
one could say who was good, who bad,
who was a sinner, who a saint,
but those He saw were saved in death
and share one grave beneath His land.

With Blood on his Hands, Commissar Y. Raichman Ponders the Forest of the Dead at Katyn, 1943

A Nazi lie and Hitler's plot?—
The forest sighs but gives no answers.
Twelve thousand Polish officers rot,
grandsons of Sobieski's lancers,
reactionary anti-Semites,
too dead to reach for thoughts or guns,
or, in the fragrant dark of spring nights,
to father patriotic sons.

Koniuchy, Eastern Poland, 1944

Perhaps there are real angels who assist
the ghosts of martyrs to the other side,
since what is left behind cannot resist
the flames of hell? A family of three died
slowly at the hands of hateful men,
and Yaakov Prenner, holding match and gas,
looks at the residue of pain: a ten
inch block of wood lodged in the father's ass,
skin peeled from the mother's neck and back,
brain matter from the infant on the floor.
He knows the enemy will soon attack,
and that if caught he won't survive the war.
In Yiddish he commands his men to pour,
to strike, and like Lot, never to look back.

Saint Bartholomew's Church
Szobiszowice/Petersdorf

1241

Stone by stone
in the name of the Lord,
with blood and bone,
with lance and sword,

the Templars build
their little church,
while in the field
the Mongols lurch,

and blowflies buzz
above the hill
of what once was
another kill.

Two arrows wan
a slanted eye;
a young *noyan*
prepares to die.

1945

Centuries
have passed. We thank
our destinies
no Soviet tank

or errant round
in one hit razes
it to the ground.
Sunlight blazes

upon its steeple,
even as cries
from local people
fill the skies.

Heaped in carts near
its buttressed walls,
they've only fear
to break their falls.

GLEIWITZ, 1945

A boy of thirteen wears the pitch black pants
of German scouts. Some women look with glee
and try to drown his cries. They curse in chants.
They're Jewish guards from State Security
who are too full of hate to want to hear
that he's too young to be a Nazi, his face
the hairless face of innocence, a tear
on his cheek his only shield. And still, they race
to pock his tender flesh with cigarettes,
delighting Lilith-like in the cruel scene.
They almost feel the pangs of something higher,
but they have come this far without regrets:
They douse his light blond hair with gasoline
and free him with the mercy of their fire.

SOMEWHERE OVER GERMANY, 1945

At the gates of heaven
he did not know the names
beyond the bombing bay.

But many miles away
he could still see the flames
judging the dead in Dresden.

Veteran's Hospital

Some nights are never-ending hells
for these old veterans in our care.
We do not hand out pills, but shells,
as out of battlefields they stare
from over sixty years ago
on far-off Guam or Guadalcanal.
With trembling hands they try to show
how the bravest or youngest fell.
We console them with a cold cup,
and a tender tap on the shoulder.
What haunts them, though, will not give up,
nor the fallen boys grow older.

PART THREE

PART THREE

AFTER THE EXPULSIONS
Gleiwitz, 1946

The old Romanesque church in Petersdorf,
closed since the Germans left the neighbourhood,
crumbles in the pouring acid rain.
Above, no bells toll for its dead; but stain
upon stain marks the stones where Mary's scarf
rests at the bare feet of its heavy rood.

EZRA POUND ENTERS THE TENT

No, this is not a station in the metro,
this is an open cage outside of Pisa.
Ezra Pound now sits inside of it,
his beard a burning bush of grief made new.
Gazing at the moon, and looking retro,
the better craftsman grins to bars, and sees a
night of stars implode, his touched eyes lit
and posed for labour. If not he, then who
will scribble truth into a timeless croon?
Twenty-five days will pass before the good
guys offer him a tent, his face now wood,
his psyche worn by rain and sun and moon.
He leaves the cage, and is assisted in,
his mouth ajar, his grin not quite a grin.

Dissident, 1962
After Josif Brodsky

Outside the window January flees
and through a web of prison cells you hear
fellow prisoners singing through the bars:
"Once again, a brother's been set free."

You can still hear their voices floating by,
and the echoing steps of stone-faced guards.
You sing yourself, sing in spite of fear:
"January, bid us all goodbye."

Facing the window, back against the door,
you drink the warm narcotic of the air.
But your thoughts grope the narrow corridor

and from one trial to the next you lurch
until you make it to that land where there's
no January, February, March.

Poland, New Year's Day, 1982

The final snow of the year, riddled and hard,
assailed by wind and rain, still covers the field,
while heaven above, a milky upturned ashtray,
lingers like a promise never fulfilled.

Smoke rises past the limbs of walking trees
toward blocks of flats that are a thousand greys.
Coal miners cough laments down muddy streets
to greasy taverns, and in shop displays

Christmas trees thirst for drink in dented pots.
Coal hills lie waiting for ice picks and shovels
as flocks of children drag ramshackle sleds
toward the toppled ruins of Eskimo hovels.

And at the roadside shelter Jesus sleeps
in the cradle of his weeping mother's arms,
the light that leaks through small cracks in the roof—
forsaken as the sparrows that chant him psalms.

A Hater Learns About Love

After a long night of interrogation,
followed by a thirty-minute trial,
there was no doubt about it: I was guilty.

So with my teeth tucked in my bleeding mouth,
and with my jaw now wired tightly shut,
a guard named Peter met me at the gate.

Looking different than I had imagined,
he smiled and kicked me point blank in the balls,
then led me like a drunkard down the stairs.

The long dark corridor seemed like a tunnel,
one with no light to mitigate the end,
only a special cell the saint made clear

was for the good, the freedom of us all.

THE LONELIEST MAN

"My coming to England [sic] in this way is, as I realize, so unusual that nobody will easily understand it. I was confronted by a very hard decision. I do not think I could have arrived at my final choice unless I had continually kept before my eyes the vision of an endless line of children's coffins with weeping mothers behind them, both English and German, and another line of coffins of mothers with mourning children."

—Rudolf Hess to his wife Ilse, June 10, 1941

He had fought in the trenches, watched the rats
gnawing the feet of dead or dying soldiers,
the flower of Europa slain in youth.
He understood Trakl's pain, the grandsons who
would never father future generations.
So the mission in his mind was clear:
he climbed into the cockpit of a fighter
and flew to Scotland. Ankle broken now,
parachute on the ground, he babbled to
a farmer, to Lord Churchill. Neither listened.
They declared him mad, and locked him up
inside the tower of London, where the rooks
of war besieged his mind, and where the clouds
brought back memories of his Grecian mother.
At Nuremberg his final words were: "I
have no regrets." He would repeat them how
many times in his cell at Spandau prison
as years turned into decades and he found
himself the lone remaining prisoner?

Towards the end, he'd whisper to pale flowers,
glance at Erich Honecker's grey portrait,
the covers of East German TV guides,
senile, limping, propped up by a cane,
a friendless, shunned, and isolated man.
When the guards found him in the summer garden
a power cord was wrapped around his neck.

THE DEATH OF COMMUNISM
Poland, 1989

Grey clouds in early May,
a hint or threat of rain.
Beyond the tracks a lane,
a bench along the way.

Night watchmen, empty tins
of bargain lager, stars
in smoke, East German cars
with soot on their tail fins.

A little further on—
unheard of graves, hedgerows,
and flocks of hooded crows
delighting in the dawn.

BUKOVINA, 1989

The peasant man still burns his leaves
which rise into Romania's skies
like smouldering stars above its eaves.
With grubby hands he shields his eyes,

but cannot stop the acrid tears
from flowing down his ruddy cheeks.
The sum and meaning of his fears
are in the yellow smoke that reeks.

His bale of hay receives a tine,
his scrawny hound a fleshless husk,
while in his sty a greedy swine
wades in the slop of early dusk.

Part Four

Part Four

Sarajevo Sonnet

Within the four walls of this sonnet's form
(while outside spring rain gathers in a pail),
there is at least one happy story to tell,
something lovely brought on by a storm.

Fresh thrifts have sprouted, and a fat worm
lazily crawls out of someone's cracked bell,
crawls out of the centre of someone's hell,
out of a skull atop a uniform,

while not too far away, in someone's rib cage,
in a sunlit temple without a steeple,
two tiny beetles in the place of people,

(their love too pure to ever turn into rage,
too tried and true to ever fail or falter),—
take their vows before a priestless altar.

Draza Bregovich

His pockets full of poems, fingers stained
from packs of Camels, green eyes wet from tears,
Draza Bregovich looks from the plane,
forgetting where he'd lived for twenty years.

America was free, but he could never
master its tongue, his phrases always strange,
his Balkan humour neither wry nor clever,
his sad and off-beat verses lacking range.

He stares out at the Alps and Italy,
lost in the composition of a line,
and then he sees the Adriatic sea,
and Montenegrin hills of spruce and pine.

When at last he sets down in Belgrade,
two plain-clothes agents greet him; crows take wing;
dust burns in his eyes; and memories fade;
yet Draza Bregovich begins to sing.

Epiphany

A mackerel sky, a blood-orange sun,
and leaves drooping from the black limbs of oaks;
and thieving magpies, hell-mirroring rooks,
behind an old woman's whispers and sighs—
sooty bricks with barbs around her heart
as she limps by, and I stop to jot it down.

Elegy

After the tears, heartfelt tears and crocodile tears,
I sit here with mouldy bread crumbs, dill leaves and salt.

The plastic clock above the fridge strikes the hour
to the sound of the same old quarrelling in the street,

echoes resound in the gutters like bits of truth
and madness still propels our globe like the first ache.

We've buried you the way you asked: with no stone
or wooden cross above your decaying forehead,

only the simple sky, the clouds, and the old sun.
And at night the moon and the stars will comfort you

more faithfully than any human ever could.
Sad grand poet, I wish I could find the right words,

but for the thousandth time the cold wind says it best,
and nothing is more eloquent than its goodbye.

BUTUGYCHAG
Eastern Siberia

From this hillside full of multiple graves
(marked by discs made from the lids of tin cans,
rusty now, stamped with the ID numbers
of Tsarist and reactionary slaves),
some with their inhabitants' remains
exposed to heaven, as if halfway risen,

we look down at the commandant's old house,
past the howls in the cramped punishment cells,
as the wind brushes bent and brambled bars,
behind which stand the spectres of those who,
before the Great Patriotic War,
sinned against the state in dreams and whispers,

and we behold the spacious balcony,
the broken panes of the enormous window,
and the sun-bleached, rain-worn wood of the stair,
built for the little man from the Ukraine
who liked to sing in Russian and in Yiddish,
because, we are told, he enjoyed the view there.

Gulag Burial Marker
Eastern Siberia

In a graveyard on a hill near Magadan,
the heavens shed light on the skull and bones
of what looks like a halfway-risen man,

a poet or a priest who died a slave,
and, buried underneath dry brush and stones,
lay for decades in a makeshift grave.

But now he lingers in a paradise
of brambleberries, nettles, pines, and cones,
with shadows in the sockets of his eyes,

as if to show he doesn't want to wake,
as if he wished to let out yet more moans,
and to protest against the wooden stake,

the crimson star, the absence of a cross,
the way, the truth, the light that mock his loss.

The Abandoned Station

Here the shades of rust are manifold.
The rails resemble velvet, thick and plush.
A dark grease from the time of the last Tsar
rests deep within the wood of sunken ties.

The platform's still, the station name in bold
Gothic letters. No pale mothers rush
their children to the last departing car
with brusque farewells forever in their eyes.

The car rusts at the edge. Has been there since
the day the Soviets sacked the sleepy town,
leaving a trail of bleeding girls and grief.

The station is a graveyard. Cleanse and rinse
it with your mind, and still a deep red brown
keeps it behind: thorn tree and nettle leaf.

The Last Silesian

Above us: cawing rooks and grey clouds.
Around us: leafless trees and falling snow.
It's late in January, 60 years
since Gleiwitz-Petersdorf was liberated.

Anne, a frail and tiny woman of eighty,
and the last Silesian on our street,
points her left hand toward the frozen ground
and rests her right upon a walking stick.

—"When Stalin's army came, the NKVD
tortured, raped and massacred our people.
Both of my parents were among the dead
buried here inside a mass grave."—

In her sad voice there are hints of dialect.
—"Later on, Poles from the East exhumed them,
planted trees, and built this lovely park."—
The dialect of the dead, and the vanquished.

An Interview with the Oldest Man in Europe

Amid the leaves of this his final Fall
his eyes reflect the blue unminding heavens,
but tell me nothing of the girl he wed
while serving in the Tsar's Imperial Guard,

tell me nothing of the six sons she bore
during the Great War and Revolution,
and nothing of the hellish years he spent,
a prisoner-slave in Kolyma's mines.

Like Midas, all he touches turns to gold—
the leaves are fallen sons and memories,
the numbers on his wrist his gilded name.

He is too close to death to answer questions.
Three died for Hitler, and three died for Stalin.
And he was cursed to have survived them all.

The Łemko Steeple

Over the valley, down into the wood,
where water laps the boulder-dotted banks,
a raven soars beneath the summer sun.
The elder *chłopi* say none have appeared
for many seasons, having understood
at last the ways of man. For on the flanks
of the old hill, no hare or vole had run
across the plush green grasses. Drought had seared
the soil; and industry had promised gain.
The young and able have moved far away,
and now the hamlet is bereft of people,
the houses bare or full of rotting hay.
The lone hope is to wait for acid rain,
or for a sign above the Łemko steeple.

STARLESS

I fingered the bone, and traced
where the axe had landed,
imagining the face
of the girl, her life abandoned
by the midnight sky.
So I placed an aster
in her tiny skull
where a glimmering eye
had been, and then I asked her
to please forgive us all.

PART FIVE

A Plurality of Worlds

Intensities of pain—
of those once persecuted
and those once executed.

The scientific gain
belongs to us, but who knows
of Giordano Bruno's

suffering on the square,
tongue-tied on cobble stone,
as he met fire alone?

Around him everywhere:
wine spilt amid the jeering,
grimaces and cheering,

squeals from a paederast,
smiles from thieving hawkers,
bishops, whores, and gawkers.

—"Into the Tiber, cast
his ashes!"—could be heard,
"for every wicked word."

WATER

Burnt Sudanese earth under claw,
a vulture waits three steps behind
a girl who crouches, strands of straw
beneath her lowered head, her mind

in refuge on the dream-kissed shores
of an oasis, where green palm
leaves shade black brows, and water pours
into a pool that's bright but calm.

A flame-tree sheds no grief, instead
droops in the backdrop. A stump lies
resembling a lion's head
still warding off the thirst of flies.

THE POET OF 1912

Where is he now, the poet of
1912? Did he go the way
of Zeppelins that flew above
the Kaiser's sky of *Soldat* grey,

his tome forgotten in the attic
of Wilhelmstrasse 13, dust
thick on its cover like the static
of yellowed years? Or did he thrust

himself into a muddy trench
as salvos burst near the latrine,
filling his nostrils with the stench
of urine, feces, and gangrene?

No matter now. He lies beneath
unconquered soil, aloof to all,
with only dust between his teeth,
and only midnight in his skull.

Anonymous Rex

"The death of a man is like the
fall of a mighty nation..."
—Czesław Miłosz

He lies beneath a stone
that weighs more than a ton,
his skull and skeleton
like ruins left alone

for twenty hundred springs,
the ruins of a temple
in which a once great people
no longer prays or sings,

their destinies and wills
vanished with each god,
their pantheon forgot
when lowered with the hills.

How to Get There

Follow the moss
along the wall;
read the language
of the cracks;
pay attention
to the rooks
cursing the clouds
above your head;
hear the tolls
of bells across
the sooty red bricks
of Petersdorf;
and watch the leaves
departing lindens,
sailing over
the iron gate
to lie among
the faded letters,
the withered flowers
and toppled stones.

PART SIX

Spreading Democracy
Serbia 1999

I.

How to explain?
Suddenly
she lies in pain
amid debris—

orphaned fingers,
blood-stained blouse—
a scream that lingers
in her razed house.

A girl who talks
to bleeding palms—
around her blocks
and carpet bombs.

II.

A pilot shrouds
the truth and smiles
amid the clouds
three hundred miles

back home to base.
He cannot tell

which was whose face.
High over hell,

his stealth's black wings
still mock the night,
and fallen things
in morning light.

Jenin, 2002

The leaves take flight this autumn
like rumours from the past.
The first rot at the bottom
of heaps hushed by the last.

THE TERRORIST

Only six, she stands before a tank,
looking at its armour, while inside
soldiers heed orders from a higher rank.
There isn't any place for her to hide,
no door to head for, no abandoned car
to slide beneath. Pure terror rules her land.
When finally crushed, she rises past the star
of David, with a stone clutched in her hand.

After the Old Masters

The father looks up to the sky or ceiling
(beyond the grey scale of the photograph)
with his son wrapped inside his cradling arms.
An orderly obscures the boy's midsection,
with silence says he is beyond all healing.
Outside the frame in colour copter strafe
restokes the ire of Taliban gendarmes
who soothe the mother twisted in dejection.
We do not catch a whiff of her pained retching,
catch sight of their clenched fists or hear their words.
We see the father's sorrow-stricken eyes
in what could almost be a Rembrandt etching,
his pitch black pupils focused heavenwards
to where God's justice or His mercy lies.

No Flowers, No Doves

When we entered the burning city
charred corpses greeted us.
A child's hand dangled from a scorched tree
and the twisted wreckage of a bus
mocked the stillness of the sky.
Gunner gagged, Ski scratched his head,
neither understanding why
he had to liberate the dead.

Two Dates

Give this soldier two dates, and engrave
them on the cold face of a lasting tomb.
They will not tell of what he lost and gave,
nor how he lived and was beloved by all
back in the little town from which he came,
nor how, inside a foxhole all alone,
he curled up like a foetus in the womb
when the sniper's bullet called his name
and, like a judgment to be writ in stone,
found him neither cowardly nor brave.

On the Beheading of
Eugene Olin Armstrong

His was not only one more tale of death
read and forgotten by the end of day.
This time I clicked the link, and short of breath,
watched a trembling man begin to pray
as five armed militants with hooded faces
announced the sentence that would end his life,
(a life spent building homes in far-off places).
But God forgive if I recall the knife
cutting through his larynx, neck and spine,
the awful hollow noises of his lungs,
the ghostless whimper of his final whine,
though to the left of him the morning sun
rushed through the curtain from the window-pane,
and angels pleaded with the wind in vain.

The July Sun Over Lebanon

She hears bombs raze the nunnery.
She hears F-16s on their way
back to Israel, to reload
new bombs sent from America.
Blinding smoke burns in her eyes
and shrouds the limbs of terrorists,
boys and girls from grammar school
who in the spring first learned to count.

On the Lynching of Saddam Hussein

"To die not knowing why is to die like an animal . . . To die like a human being you have at least got to know why it is done to you."
—Ezra Pound

You hear your lungs begin to rattle.
This is the rattle mother told
you about: it comes before your death
    as vital organs fail.

It is the end of agonizing
suffocation, when life puts
a pillow on your nose and mouth.
    All death is suffocation.

Indifferent light penetrates
the jello in your bedside bowl,
and hell absorbs the fluorescent bulb's
    impalpable low heat.

You died with tubes inside your mouth,
gasping for one more breath of air,
your fragile fists still clenched in fear
    before almighty Allah.

No mercenary's noose was placed
around your neck, as round Saddam's.
You did not chasten craven tormentors,
   falling through the gallows.

BLACK OPS

No, there are no black helicopters
hovering over every breath.
And yet: are there forensic doctors
who can confirm Osama's death?

No, there is no rich one percent,
no Bleistein smoking his cigar,
no swelling ghettos or dissent,
no Soros watching from afar.

No, there is no new world order,
no US president that lied.
And yet in Gaza there is murder,
and few know how Gaddafi died.

Part Seven

A Warning to Dissidents

Yes, pretty soon now they'll be at your door.
They've orders and a warrant after all.
It doesn't matter. You'll be on the floor,
your wife and children having watched you fall.

Just then you'll notice fallen scraps and crumbs,
the beauty of your startled wife's pale feet,
the Celtic Crosses on your daughter's thumbs,
the food above that you will never eat.

Your thoughts will have become a crimson pond
that flows out of your gagged and bleeding head
until you find yourself afloat, beyond
the reach of billy clubs and flying lead.

HALLOWEEN, 2006

You see October at the foot of hills,
the leaves of suburbs rotting in the yards
of smiling couch-potatoes, hands on hearts
that beat because they can. They've made their wills.
They will bequeath their kingdoms and their money
to bunny shelters. Childless, they will send
their love to Bantu tribesmen, give the honey
from their jars to geisha girls who bend
and make their beds. Yes, you can smell the rot
as you see young men dressed as Catholic nuns
parade the streets, young women crude and worn
by buck abuse, and yahoos watching, fraught
with fear, and waving flags. The evil runs
its course. A rough beast slouches to be born.

THE CONDEMNED HOUSE
After a Black & White Photograph by Jared Carter

Who alive remembers who lived there
seventy years ago? A family
of WASPs set in their ways? The leafless tree
in front was just a sapling then. Despair
did not weigh heavy on the owner's brow,
a man who paid his taxes, loved his wife,
and who in '44 gave up his life
for freedom? Who today cares or knows how?
And now the house is boarded up, its last
tenants peddlers of cheap crack cocaine,
its naked boards exposed to elements,
its roof's tar-paper caught in the grey blast,
around it dirty snow, above it rain.
The photo knows itself what it laments.

Understanding the Holocaust

She looks outside and can no more pretend
she does not see her country getting darker.
She's lived here all her life, but she can't mend
the neighbourhood. The news is even starker.
Last night some men burned down old Nelly's place,
just after raping her as punishment
for being white. She hears it wasn't race
related, yet who pauses to lament
the woman murdered by the savages?
She stands beside her locked and bolted door
and she attempts to fathom the disease
by its symptoms, sighing at the damages
inflicted on the working-class and poor,
and sirens only add to her unease.

Vision

After the apocalypse the bodies
of both the saved and damned lay blown to bits
on the four corners of the smouldering earth,

waiting for a god to mete out justice,
but he too lay among the rotting corpses,
a trillion myths and dreams his resting bed.

Only the most resilient of the mammals,
the lowly rat, cared to attend the wake,
devouring the limbs of both the good and bad.

And then the winter came to shroud the skulls
and skeletons of both the true believers
and those who lived with very little faith.

And in the night, the particles of snow
on their exposed ribs mirrored glimmering stars.

Monomatapa on the Detroit River

When the fair-skinned missionaries came,
they were struck by the beauty of the ruins.
The heathen natives, living in crude huts now,
told them vaguely of a mighty kingdom
where Hannibal and Cleopatra ruled.
This was a city of bronze architects,
of bronze philosophers and of bronze poets.
The graffiti on the walls were hieroglyphs,
and the railway station Malcolm's palace.

EPILOGUE

Epilogue

Although the end seems near
(your neighbourhood and race
gone to the dogs), my dear,

dear reader—do not cower
in fear; stand up and face
the dogs!   In you the power

remains to save the West.
Put down your childless Spengler
who spawned two books at best.

Better to heed the deeds
of a forsaken prisoner
like Hess, or charge on steeds

like John Sobieski, steady
in soul; to follow Lee's
Rebs into battle, ready

for a certain death,
than to live on with fleas
upon your blood and breath.

About the Author

Leo Yankevich was born into a family of Roman Catholic Irish-Polish immigrants on October 30, 1961. He grew up and attended high school in Farrell, Pennsylvania, a small steel town in the Rust Belt of middle America. He then studied History and Polish at Alliance College, Cambridge Springs, Penn., receiving a BA in 1984. Later that year he travelled to Poland on a fellowship to study at the centuries-old Jagiellonian University in Krakow. A staunch anticommunist, he played an active role in the dissident movement in that country, and was arrested and beaten badly on a few occasions by the communist security forces. After the fall of the Iron Curtain in 1989, he decided to settle permanently in Poland. Since that time he has lived in Gliwice (Gleiwitz), an industrial city in Upper Silesia.

www.ingramcontent.com/pod-product-compliance
Lightning Source LLC
Chambersburg PA
CBHW021020090426
42738CB00007B/842